Norfolk B

A guide to the bea

Steve & Alyson Appleyard

Red Flannel Publishing

Dedication

This book is dedicated to our grandchildren Maisie, Zak, George, Lily, Oscar and Amelia who added to the enjoyment of the beaches.

Published in 2009 by Red Flannel Publishing, Plumtree House Mill Lane, East Runton, Norfolk, NR27 9PH

www.norfolkguides.co.uk

ISBN 978-0-9561346-0-8

Printed by Barnwell Print Ltd, Aylsham, Norfolk

CONTENTS

The beaches are numbered 1 to 50 in a clockwise direction around the coast starting with "West of King's Lynn". They are also shown on the ouline of the coast on the following two pages.

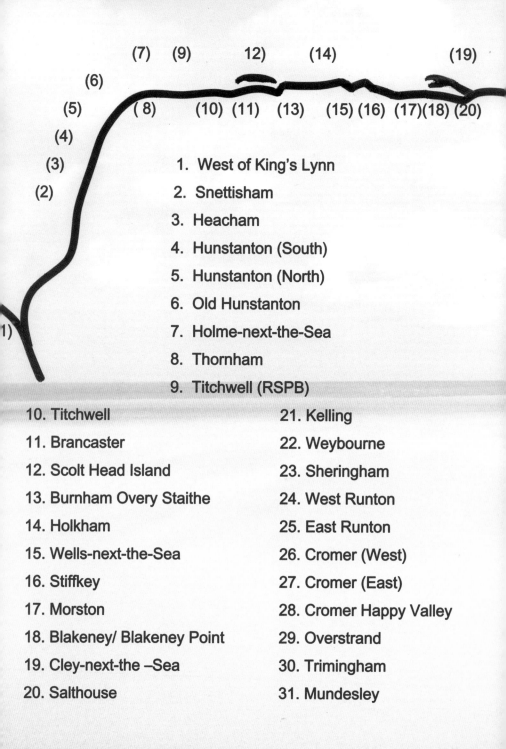

(7) (9)   12)   (14)   (19)

(6)

(5)   (8)   (10) (11)   (13)   (15) (16) (17)(18) (20)

(4)

(3)   1. West of King's Lynn

(2)   2. Snettisham

            3. Heacham

            4. Hunstanton (South)

            5. Hunstanton (North)

            6. Old Hunstanton

1)   7. Holme-next-the-Sea

            8. Thornham

            9. Titchwell (RSPB)

10. Titchwell	21. Kelling
11. Brancaster	22. Weybourne
12. Scolt Head Island	23. Sheringham
13. Burnham Overy Staithe	24. West Runton
14. Holkham	25. East Runton
15. Wells-next-the-Sea	26. Cromer (West)
16. Stiffkey	27. Cromer (East)
17. Morston	28. Cromer Happy Valley
18. Blakeney/ Blakeney Point	29. Overstrand
19. Cley-next-the –Sea	30. Trimingham
20. Salthouse	31. Mundesley

(22) (23)

21)   (24) (2 5)

(26,27)   (28)

(29) (30)

32. Bacton   (31)   (32)

33. Walcott   (33)   (34)

34. Happisburgh   (35)   (36)

35. Eccles-on-Sea   (37)   (38)

36. Sea Palling   (39)

37. Waxham   (40)

38. Waxham Sands   (41)

39. Horsey   (42)

40. Winterton-on-Sea   (43)

41. Hemsby   (44)

42. Newport   (45)

43. Scratby   (46)

44. California   (47)

45. Caister-on-Sea   (48)

46. Great Yarmouth (North)   (49)

47. Great Yarmouth (South)   (50)

48. Gorleston-on-Sea (North)

49. Gorleston-on-Sea (South)

50. Hopton-on-Sea

Beach Code

Much of the Norfolk coast is a Special Area of Conservation and a European Marine Site which means that special care must be taken when visiting these areas. The seashore code should always be observed.

Try to leave everything as you find it.
Avoid sand dunes, saltmarsh and cliffs - they are sensitive environments and vulnerable to erosion. Keep to established footpaths and boardwalks. Tread carefully on the shoreline to avoid disturbing or damaging rockpools and marine life. Respect our coastline and other users. Supervise children at all times. Keep dogs under control - remember its is illegal to disturb or harass many species of birds and other animals.
Keep seashore activities away from birds' summer breeding grounds and winter roosts - for example, kite flying can be particularly alarming to birds. Stay clear of the main bird roosts between 1st October and 31st March and the summer breeding grounds between 1st April and 31st July.
Avoid disturbing wintering birds during cold spells – at these times they must feed whenever possible and conserve their energy,
Reduce the risk of fire by not lighting fires, stoves or barbecues.
Please take your litter home.
Off - road driving on the seashore and seawalls is not permitted.

Also remember that the seashore can be a dangerous place -
Keep a close eye on children - the sea is a dangerous place.
It is advisable not to take inflatables into the sea -exercise extreme caution and always tie them to the shore.
Check tide times to avoid being cut off and keep a close eye on incoming tides.
Stay away from soft mud, quicksand, slippery rocks, creeks and cliffs.
Observe local beach safety information and byelaws. Watch out for local hazards.
Back fill any holes. Do not dig in sensitive habitats such as sand dunes or saltmarsh.
For further information and advice contact - The Wash and North Norfolk Coast

Introduction

In the summer of 2008 we explored the Norfolk coast with the aim of visiting every beach. On some occasions we had grandchildren with us and so we could observe the enjoyment that they experienced. In other cases the pleasure was totally ours, particularly when we visited the many beaches that have an abundance of wildlife. Whether you are looking for a beach for seaside activities with your family, to walk the dog or simply to sit and watch the ships go by, we hope that you will find this guide helpful.

Having visited and enjoyed Norfolk over many years we chose to retire here and enjoy what we knew to be an exceptional coastline. Having now seen it all, from vast sandy beaches, through cliffs, shingle banks, sand dunes and open marshes we are even more firmly of the view that the Norfolk coast is unrivalled.

Steve & Alyson Appleyard

1 West of King's Lynn

We have to start this guide with an admission that there are not actually fifty beaches in Norfolk but only forty-nine. The last beach when travelling westward along the Norfolk coast is at Snettisham, but we were curious as to what lay beyond and for the sake of completeness we wanted to start our journey at the Norfolk/Lincolnshire boundary. The coastal county border is on the south-western side of the Wash between the rivers Ouse and Nene and fortunately there is a footpath which runs along the top of the outer sea wall.

The view from the path is of saltmarsh and tidal flats which makes up the largest National Nature Reserve in England. It has been notified as a site of Special Scientific Interest and has been designated as a Natura 2000 site under the European Union Birds and Habitats Directive. It is also designated as a Ramsar site under the Convention on Wetlands of International Importance. Even if we don't understand what all this means, we can deduce it is a special place and as the information boards go on to say -" The Wash is one of England's last great wilderness areas". The extensive area of open water, mud, sand and saltmarsh supports an enormous number of plants and animals adapted to live in the ebb and flow of the tide. The Wash supports internationally important numbers of geese and wading birds which feed on the saltmarsh and organisms living in the mud.

1 West of King's Lynn

The footpath can be accessed from King's Lynn via the ferry across the Ouse to West Lynn and continues for ten miles to a car park and picnic area at the mouth of the Nene. There is also a car park after 3.5 miles at Ongar Hill which is reached via Terrington St Clement. The path on the sea wall is known as

the Peter Scott Walk - as a tribute to Scott's work for conservation and his role as founder of the Wildfowl and Wetlands Trust. Peter Scott lived in a lighthouse, which is at the Nene end of the walk, from 1933 to 1939. A manmade island two miles from the mouth of the River Nene was built in 1975 as part of a study into the building of

four large freshwater reservoirs and has now been designated as a Seabird Nesting Reserve. Given the length of the full walk it is worth finding a friend who will drop you off at the lighthouse and then meet you at West Lynn, or as you get off the ferry in Ferry Lane in King's Lynn (the ferry crosses every 20 minutes). The photograph at the top of the previous page shows the view (taken with a telephoto lens) across the marshes and the mouth of the Ouse to Hunstanton. While there is the occasional boardwalk that leads into the marshes, these are probably for use by wildfowlers and it is strongly advised that you do not venture into the marshes, as you will be disturbing the wildlife as well as risking your own life.

2 Snettisham

Snettisham is the first place on the Wash which has a beach and is the nearest destination for those heading to the coast along the A47. The beach is almost two miles from the A148 and the village of Snettisham. The turning into Beach Road is well signed and there is a large car park at the very end of the road as it arrives at the beach. The car park is close to a caravan park, summer shops and cafés and toilets. The beach is a mix of stone and sand, with grassy areas behind. As with other places on the Wash the tide goes out a huge distance, leaving an expanse of wet sand and mud. In many places the mud becomes ankle deep just a short distance from the beach. As well as the caravans there is a row of privately owned holiday bungalows facing seawards.

2 Snettisham

At the southern end of Snettisham beach is the RSPB Snettisham Nature Reserve, as you walk along the path you will come to bird hides which you can use without having to be a member. From the hides you can enjoy one of the country's greatest wildlife spectacles, when rising high spring tides force thousands of birds to leave the mudflats where they are feeding and settle close to the hides. Just inland of the beach are a series of lakes formed from disused gravel pits. Some are part of the RSPB reserve and others are used by members of the Snettisham Beach Sailing Club.

3 Heacham

Heacham has two sandy beaches, designated as North and South Beach. North beach has a wide promenade behind which are beach huts. South beach is wider and is backed by sand dunes. The tide recedes a considerable distance leaving a wide strip of wet sand providing spectacular vistas.

3 Heacham

There are car parks at both beaches, the larger being at the North Beach. You cannot drive directly between the two beaches, but you have to take the appropriate road from the village centre. As you approach the South Beach you cross the attractive Heacham River which is parallel to the coast. The

Indian Princess Pocahontas who married John Rolfe a local Heacham squire, is depicted on the village sign. Heacham is associated with Norfolk lavender and a visit to Caley Mill the nearby lavender farm and centre is recommended.

4 Hunstanton (South)

The southern part of Hunstanton's beach is all about fun. As far as we have seen, this is the only beach in Norfolk where you can ride a pony or donkey. The firm sand is great for cricket and the pools around the groins are an eternal attraction for children. Digging holes and making sandcastles occupy children for hours on end. The tide goes out some distance but this doesn't deter people from walking across the firm wet sand for a paddle or a swim.

Behind the beach is a traditional promenade along which you can simply stroll and take in the sea air, or you can partake of the many exciting rides, or visit the Oasis Leisure Centre or the Sea Life Sanctuary. A particularly memorable way to spend your time is to take one of the Searles sea tours. Searles

operate amphibious vehicles from the promenade. Some of the trips take you along the shoreline and are accompanied by an interesting commentary. Others link up with their boat the Sealion, which takes you across the Wash to sandbanks to see basking seals.

5 Hunstanton (North)

The north beach at Hunstanton must be the most instantly recognisable of all the Norfolk beaches , with its distinctive brown and white striped cliffs and large rounded stones. This is the quieter end of what is a popular seaside holiday and day visit destination and the beach is a key feature of the resort.

5 Hunstanton (North)

The 18m high cliffs at Hunstanton are made up of three contrasting rock strata, white chalk, red chalk and the base layer of Carrstone. Carrstone has been used as a building material for houses in this part of Norfolk for generations. The cliffs, which are constantly eroding, are apparently a very good place to find fossils and they are recognised as a geological site of importance. While there is much written about the cliffs, we could not find anything about the smooth stones on this part of the beach. The curious aspect is their regular formation when viewed from the

promenade. If anyone can throw any light on this, we would be pleased to hear from you. Another curiosity on the beach is the remains of the old trawler Sheraton. It was going to be used as a target boat in the Wash when it ran ashore in 1946. The ship was cut up and salvaged in the 1950's leaving just the remaining bottom part of the hull.

5 Hunstanton (North)

On the cliff top is a large car park with excellent views of the beaches of Hunstanton and Old Hunstanton and on a clear day you can see across the Wash to the Lincolnshire coast. Also on the cliff top is a lighthouse now a private dwelling and the ruins of St Edmunds Chapel which dates back to

1272 and celebrates the visit by St Edmund in 855. Hunstanton is the start of the Norfolk Coast Path which joins with the Peddars Way at Holme-next-the-Sea. Hunsanton was created by the land owning Le Strange family of Old Hunstanton. Henry Styleman Le Strange had the vision of

building a coastal holiday village. The Golden Lion Hotel was the first building which was completed in 1846. Development accelerated when the railway came to Hunstanton in 1862. The work was continued by his son who took the development beyond the original vision and turned it into the attractive resort that you see today.

5 Hunstanton (North)

Hunstanton is unique as an east coast resort in that it faces west and so the sun sets over the sea. The sunsets can be long and spectacular, the one that we observed in mid September certainly was.

6 Old Hunstanton

The beach at Old Hunstanton is owned by the Le Strange family - the family who were responsible for the creation of "new" Hunstanton. It is a delightful beach with extensive sand dunes as well as wide open beaches and is totally uncommercialised, in contrast with its neighbour.

6 Old Hunstanton

At Old Hunstanton the cliffs of the eastern part of Hunstanton reduce in height and finally disappear into the sand dunes. There is a large car park from which there is a short walk to the beach, passing a pleasant looking café and through a gap in the dunes. Within the dunes are beach huts of a variety of sizes and colours. We did notice that when the tide comes in, islands are formed and care should be taken to avoid becoming stranded. The Le Strange Old Barn craft shop and art gallery is on the road down to the beach and is well worth a visit.

7 Holme-next-the-Sea

We could have treated Holme beach as two separate beaches. There is the beach directly at the end of Beach Road and the beach further east which runs alongside the Holme Dunes Nature Reserve. Beach Road is a turning off the A149 to the west of the village of Holme. There is a car park, refreshments and toilets at the end of the road and the beach is a short walk across a golf course and sand dunes. The beach is firm sand with an undulation that we noticed causes islands to form as the tide comes in. Care should be taken to avoid becoming cut off. The beach at Holme is where "Seahenge" was discovered in 1998. The 4000 year old 55 oak timber posts are now in a museum in Kings Lynn. Looking westwards you can see the cliffs at Hunstanton in the distance.

7 Holme-next-the-Sea

The Holme Dunes National Nature Reserve is reached by taking a right turn off Beach Road just prior to the beach car park. After about half a mile along this unmade road you enter the reserve and in a further half mile you reach the Norfolk Wildlife Trust visitor centre. There are a number of extremely pleasant walks through the varied habitats of the reserve including a Corsican Pine woodland. You may see some black peat beds on the beach at low tide. These are the remains of an ancient forest and you should avoid walking directly over them.

8 Thornham

The beach at Thornham is a wide area of sandflats backed by sand dunes and salt marsh. It is a most tranquil place to walk, but great care should be taken to avoid being caught by the fast incoming tide. Razor shells are a common sight along this stretch of the Norfolk Coast, and here there are

uncountable numbers washed up on the shore line. The marshes behind the beach are managed by the Norfolk Wildlife Trust and are home to a large number of birds including Redshanks, which build nests amongst the plants in such a way that they can withstand tidal flooding.

8 Thornham

You can reach the beach from a small car park at the harbour which is accessed from Staithe Lane, a turning off the A149 at the western end of the village. A land mark at this small quay on the creek is the 18th century coal barn, which floods at high spring tides. The beach is reached by walking along

the embankment from the car park, but you must look out for a turn off on your right after about three quarters of a mile. This will take you on a well trodden and generally dry path across Ragged Marsh and the sand dunes to the beach. Continuing along the embankment leads to the NWT centre.

9 Titchwell   RSPB Reserve

A visit to the beach here at the RSPB Titchwell Reserve should form part of a visit to this excellent nature reserve. There is good access to the beach, and a viewing platform where you can sit and watch the birds out at sea and on the shoreline. The sand dunes which edge the beach are eroding rapidly. Thirty years ago the WWII pill box was in the middle of the dunes and now it is in the middle of the beach. The walk to the beach from the RSPB car park is about one mile. It is easy walking but plenty of time should be allowed so you can visit the hides on the way.

9 Titchwell   RSPB Reserve

The entrance to the RSPB Reserve is directly off the A149 to the west of the village of Titchwell. There is a large car park, toilets, RSPB shop and an excellent café. It is one of the RSPB's most visited reserves because of the huge range of birds that can be seen here throughout the year, including our

two favourites - Marsh Harriers and Avocets. There are three nature trails - the Meadow Trail, the Fen Trail and the West Bank Trail. All the paths and hides have good accessibility. At the visitor centre are feeders on which you can usually see finches and tits.

10 Titchwell

This beach is east of the RSPB nature reserve and east of a creek which drains from the marshes to the sea. The sand is very firm in places and is ideal for activities with wheeled kite boards which appear to be allowed on this beach.

The beach is reached directly from Titchwell by walking down Gipsy Lane. The entrance to the lane is directly off the A149 just beyond the eastern edge of the village. The first part of the lane is through a copse and then it opens out onto an embankment across the marshes. After approximately half a mile you have the option of continuing on the embankment which will take you to the beach at Brancaster or you can turn off left and take a well trodden path across the marshes to the Titchwell beach shown in the photographs. The turn off point is across a bridge signed "Brancaster Ford". If you have a car, an option is to drive to the Brancaster beach car park and then walk westwards along the beach until you reach the Titchwell beach.

11 Brancaster

Brancaster is a popular beach renowned for its wide expanse of firm sand with sand dunes behind. We visited on a breezy day during the week following the school summer holidays and so it was rather quiet, but there would be plenty of space for everyone even on the busiest of days. The western end of Scolt Head Island can be seen in the distance, but you most definitely should not try to reach it by crossing the estuary. The wreck of the SS Varna is exposed at low water. Great care should be taken in the water because the tide comes in quickly and there are strong rip currents.

11 Brancaster

The turning to the beach is at the western end of Brancaster and this leads to a large beach car park with toilets and refreshments. It is a short walk to the beach past the Royal West Norfolk Golf Club.

Burnham Deepdale

The OS Explorer map shows a footpath starting at Burnham Deepdale and crossing the marshes to Scolt Head Island. We found the footpath and started off enthusiastically at low tide, but we very soon arrived at a creek which we were unable to cross. The views across the marsh were superb, we admired them and then reluctantly returned to our car.

12 Scolt Head Island

Scolt Head Island is a National Nature Reserve managed by Natural England and is described by them as "..the finest example of an offshore barrier island in the UK". It is four miles long, over 700 hectares in area and it is continuing to grow westwards. The main habitats of the reserve are sand dunes, saltmarsh and intertidal mud and salt flats. The island is used for ecological research and teaching by schools and universities. The reserve supports an internationally important breeding colony of sandwich, common and little terns. There is a fine wide beach with lots of shells.

12 Scolt Head Island

So how do you get to Scolt Head Island? The easiest way is to take the ferry which operates from Burnham Overy Staithe. However we arrived there almost by accident having walked from a small car park in the village of Burnham Norton. A well trodden footpath heads northwards from the car park across the grazing marshes and after one mile you meet the Norfolk Coast Path. At which point you can turn right to Burnham Overy Staithe or left to Burnham Deepdale. However there was also a clear path across the marshes which we followed. As it was low water and a fine clear

day we were able to walk to Scolt Head. Other people there had walked across from the beach at Burnham Overy. However on arrival at the island there was a sign which read "Do not attempt to cross between the mainland and the island at low water". It also pointed out that the island is cut off at high tide. So our recommendation is to take the ferry. The sign also said that dogs are not are not allowed from April to mid August.

13 Burnham Overy Staithe

The walk to the beach from the car park is more than one mile and is longer than at any of the other Norfolk beaches - but it is well worth the effort. The path which starts at the Staithe car park follows the Overy Creek and has grazing marshes to the east. The walking is easy, it has superb panoramic

views and it is also firm enough for cycling. You finally reach the beach on a board walk which takes you over the high sand dunes. The beach is a large expanse of soft sand with lots of shells. This is the start of the Holkham National Nature Reserve which stretches to Blakeney.

13 Burnham Overy Staithe

Burnham Overy Staithe is a popular location for sailing and fishing and for just sitting and watching all the activity. It is probable that Nelson, who was born at the nearby Burnham Thorpe, started sailing here. At low water the banks on the far side of the creek dry out and are quite sandy, so a lot of people appear to wade across to have fun. Care should be taken to avoid becoming stranded. A ferry operates between here and Scolt Head.

14 Holkham

The beach and the bay at Holkham are the centre of the Holkham National Nature Reserve which is owned by the Earl of Leicester and the Crown Estates. The Holkham Reserve stretches from Burnham Norton to Blakeney and covers some 4,000 hectares. As you walk from the car park along the boardwalk and emerge from the pinewoods you are met with the spectacular sweep of Holkham Bay, with the sea just visible in the distance. We have visited Holkham

many times over the past years but have never seen the sea cover the sand in the bay. We understand that this only happens with the highest of spring tides. The half mile walk to the sea across the bay is straightforward as the sand is firm. The curve of the bay is lined with pine trees, sand dunes and soft sand making it a sheltered and popular area to spend the day. Gwyneth Paltrow walked across Holkham sand at low tide during the closing scenes of the film "Shakespeare in Love" and local beaches also feature in BBC's "Kingdom".

14 Holkham

The parking for Holkham Bay is in Lady Ann's Drive, which is directly off the A149 opposite the main entrance to Holkham Hall. Access to the beach is directly through the pine trees, but alternatively there are many paths in the

pinewoods which provide a complete contrast to walking along the beach. We particularly enjoyed a circular walk which starts by following the Peddars Way and Norfolk Coast Path eastwards along the landward side of the pines. When you reach Wells lifeboat station you can return along the beach. This is a total distance of about four miles. There is usually a mobile snack trailer parked in Lady Anne's Drive and there is a café and restaurant within the Holkham estate.

15 Wells-next-the-Sea

We have decided that we will not be making a judgement as to which we believe to be the best of all the Norfolk beaches, but had we decided to do so then without doubt the beach at Wells would be in the top three. Its main feature is the vast area of fine sand with shallow pools which are very popular with small children.

However Wells beach is much more than a seaside resort, but is part of one of the largest Nature Reserves in the country, managed by Natural England in partnership with Holkham Estate. Together with the beach at Holkham there are four miles of white-gold sand and so even on the busiest of bank holidays it is possible to find a place to sit in complete peace and solitude.

At low water it is possible to wade across the estuary to an even more remote area of sands. There is no way to return other than back across the estuary and so it is very important if you venture across that you are not caught out by the rising tide. To warn everyone, a siren sounds after the tide has turned. The colourful beach huts are a feature of Wells beach. Each one is individual and no doubt they cost an enormous amount of money. However some are available for hire, by the day or week from the nearby Pinewoods Holiday Park. Wells beach is located in an "Area of Outstanding Natural Beauty" and you should take care to minimise the impact that you make during your visit.

15 Wells-next-the-Sea

Wells-next-the-Sea is not actually next to the sea, since the beach is almost one mile from the quay and town. You can drive directly to the large car park at the Pinewoods Holiday Park and then walk through the pine trees to the beach. This leads past the lifeboat station and across a boardwalk to the main

areas of the beach. A third option is to take the 10 $^1/_4$" gauge Wells Harbour Railway to the Pinewoods Holiday Camp. A regular service is operated from mid March until the October half term holiday. There are toilets, supermarket and coffee shop at Pinewoods.

15 Wells-next-the-Sea

Wells-next-the-Sea is both a traditional seaside town with amusement arcades and a charming and historic town with the largest harbour on the North Norfolk coast. Fishing boats still go crabbing, shrimping and whelking and a sailing ship moored at the quayside serves pancakes. Wells is a

popular holiday destination with many visitors staying at the Pinewoods Holiday Park, which is managed by the Holkham Estate. Next to Pinewoods is Abrahams Bosom, an outdoor leisure area with boating on a five acre lake and other activities including trampolining and crazy golf. This area is sheltered by a strip of Corsican pines which were planted in the 1850's.

16 Stiffkey

We have read two accounts of the "beach" at Stiffkey. One guide states "A trek across the marshes will eventually bring you to the sandy beaches of Stiffkey, the tide line is often two miles from the beach". A past article about the author Rafaella Barker in the Guardian, reports that Stiffkey is one of her favourite beaches, which she knows from living in Norfolk as a child. It also describes her family's fondness for mud sliding in the marsh creeks. We must admit that despite trying three times, we failed to get to the tide line or see sandy beaches. As you will see from the photographs, the last

time we tried was on a bright wintery day in January. On the last occasion we were beaten back by the depth of water in Cabbage Creek, which would have been above our boots, and we also encountered some sinking sand. If we had been more determined during our first summer foray we could probably have waded across the creek. However we did see an example of the creek mud sliding which Rafaella Barker's family so enjoyed. Even if we didn't get to a sandy beach, we thoroughly enjoyed our walks across the marshes, which form part of a National Trust nature reserve and onto the wet sands which stretch out into the distance beyond.

16 Stiffkey

There are two ways to get onto the marshes and then the sands beyond. The first is down Green Way which is a turning off the A149 to the west of the village. At the end of this lane is a small car park which is on the edge of the marshes. The walk across the marshes is about half a mile after which you come to a ridge of marram grass and gorse shown on the O.S. map as Stiffkey Meals. Beyond this is West Sand, a disused outfall pipe can be seen stretching into the distance. The end of this pipe is at Cabbage Creek and seals were basking on the sands beyond. The second way to the marshes is along the Bangay Green Way bridleway at the eastern end of the village.

17 Morston

Morston is a popular place for boating enthusiasts, having a very busy quay on the sheltered Morston Creek. We went to Morston knowing that it does not have a beach, but it qualifies for entry in this guide because from Morston you

can take a ferry to one of the most remote beaches in Norfolk at Blakeney Point. The boats are operated by the local companies - Beans, Bishops and Temples and they take you on hour long trips to see the seals basking on the beach at the Point. Some of the trips allow you to disembark.

There is a large grassy car park at Morston which is owned by the National Trust , who also manage the surrounding area of marshes. There is a NT visitor centre and lookout from which there are superb views of the marshes

and the many species of birds which inhabit it. Within the car park there is a small café and usually a mobile sandwich bar that sells excellent fresh crab sandwiches. As part of our search for possible beaches we walked westwards on the Norfolk Coast Path for one mile until we came to Freshes Creek (main photo on P46). This is a most pleasant walk with views of the marshes and Blakeney Point beyond. We also recommend the 1.5 mile walk eastwards to Blakeney.

18 Blakeney & Blakeney Point

Blakeney was a commercial seaport until the early 20th century but now only small boats can sail up the estuary. It is a very picturesque village with excellent restaurants and hotels and is a popular holiday and weekend destination. It does not however have a beach or access to a beach, as you cannot reach Blakeney Point directly (unless you have your own boat) - see the sections on Morston and Cley. Having said there is no beach, older children have fun on the exposed sand banks, but they have to be very careful not to be stranded when the tide comes in. Crabbing from the quayside is a popular pastime, as of course is boating. There is a large car park from which you can sit and watch all the activity on the river.

18 Blakeney & Blakeney Point

The easiest way to reach Blakeney Point is by taking one of the hour long seal trips operated for many years by local families. These all start from the adjoining village of Morston, although you buy the tickets on the quayside at Blakeney. Their advertising literature says "You are guaranteed to see the

seals" and if you are lucky to have good weather, then you will certainly have a most memorable day. Some of the trips allow you to disembark to walk around, but this is at a point some distance away from the seals.

18 Blakeney & Blakeney Point

The tough way to reach Blakeney Point is to walk the almost four miles from the NWT beach car park at Cley (turn left off the A149 just as you leave Cley heading east). It is made all the more difficult because you are for the most part walking on shingle. The

whole area is the Blakeney National Nature Reserve and is managed by the National Trust. As their literature states "..it is one of the most scenic, unspoilt and evocative places in Britain". It comprises of three main habitats - shingle, sand dunes and saltmarsh and over 260 species of birds have been recorded. The National Trust

has the difficult task of enabling people to visit and enjoy the area, while at the same time protecting a fragile landscape and its wildlife from damage. You should be very aware of this if you decide to walk to Blakeney Point and in particular avoid walking on the sand dunes which are especially fragile.

18 Blakeney & Blakeney Point

Blakeney Point is internationally important for breeding terns and parts of the Point are out of bounds in the breeding season. The area where the seals bask at high tide and are viewed from the boats are similarly excluded, but as

the tide recedes the seals move out to other islands as can just be seen in the distance in the main photograph. If you are lucky, as we were, some of the seals will swim close to the shore. The two in the photograph showed great curiosity and were only a few feet from the waters edge. The seals are a mixture of Common and Grey. More information is given about the seals, as well as the birds and the flora of Blakeney Point, in an information centre housed within the old lifeboat house. You will need to allow a full day for your walk to Blakeney Point and you should be prepared for a possible adverse change in the weather conditions.

19 Cley-next-the-Sea

The beach at Cley is part of the shingle bank which extends for some eight miles from Weybourne to Blakeney Point, but what makes this section so special is the Norfolk Wildlife Trust Cley Marsh nature reserve, which covers a large area behind the beach. The NWT's own literature is undoubtedly correct when it states "..it is one of Britain's best nature reserves for bird watching. The many hides provide spectacular views over pools and scrapes which attract water birds in

their thousands." To visit the hides you will first need to purchase a pass from the visitor centre which is on the south side of the A149 and has a large car park.The NWT's beach car park is reached by turning down the lane just as you leave Cley heading eastwards.

19 Cley-next-the-Sea

There are excellent views of Cley Marsh directly from the NWT centre (entry is free) with the advantage that you can purchase a cup of coffee or even eat lunch while watching the birds. In the spring and summer you can see

avocet, spoonbill and ringed plover amongst the many varieties and in winter the visitors include wigeon, pintail and brent geese. Our favourites, which are present all the year round are the magnificent marsh harriers. The hides are approached via boardwalks through the reeds and these give you a much closer view of the various pools and scrapes, as well as an opportunity enroute to look out for the various birds which inhabit the reeds including sedge and reed warblers.

20 Salthouse

Salthouse beach is reached by taking the right turn into Beach Road at the start of the village when arriving from the east on the A149 coast road. Beach Road takes you across Salthouse Marshes to a free car park. There is a

massive shingle ridge between the car park and the sea, although this has recently been breached by the sea in several places. The beach is totally made of pebbles and is popular with anglers. Swimming is not advised because of the strong currents. To the east of the car park is Gramborough Hill,

which is fairly inconspicuous rising to only 30m but was a Romano-British settlement and is now owned by the National Trust. A number of Roman remains have been found, suggesting that there was a pottery kiln on the site, which was more than a mile from the sea at that time.

20 Salthouse

The most notable find at Gramborough Hill, of a Roman bronze bird thought to have been part of a brooch, was made by a school boy taking part in an archaeological dig in 1980. Salthouse marshes are managed by the Norfolk

Wildlife Trust and are one of a number of important sites for birds along this section of the Norfolk Coast. There is very often a van selling coffee in the beach car park and in the village is the welcoming Dun Cow pub as well as Cookies, which is renowned for its crab and shell fish salads.

21 Kelling

When we visited the beach at Kelling only a sole angler had made the almost one mile walk from Kelling village. The shingle beach is the same as the adjoining Weybourne and Salthouse beaches which are readily accessed by

car, so unless you wish to enjoy the walk or cycle ride there is little reason to visit Kelling beach. Like its neighbours there are deep channels and strong inshore currents and so it is therefore not safe for swimming, but is ideal for angling. Meadow Lane which leads to Kelling Hard and the beach,

appears to be accessible by car but it passes over private land and unauthorised vehicles are not allowed. Kelling Hard was apparently the site of a fierce skirmish between exisemen and smugglers in the 19th Century. There is a small parking area where Meadow Lane joins the A149, near the war memorial in the village.

21 Kelling

We hope that we are not being too negative about the beach at Kelling and it is certainly not our intention to put you off visiting the area. Just the opposite, both Kelling as a village and the surrounding area are well worth exploring, including Kelling Heath, Muckleborough Hill and the local teashop/gallery.

22 Weybourne

Weybourne is the point on the coast where the cliffs end and the shingle bank which stretches to Blakeney Point starts. The waters off Weybourne are reported to be very deep and this has been a part of the coast for which there

has been a risk of invasion ever since Elizabethan times. An old rhyme states:
"He would Old England win.
Must at Weybourne Hope begin."
You can walk along the cliff top to Sheringham on what is part of the Norfolk Coast Path and Peddars Way.

The beach is reached from a turning off the A149 in Weybourne village and there is a large car park at the beach. It is popular with beach anglers because of the deep water, but swimming is not recommended because of strong undercurrents. The invasion risk at this point in the coast continued

right up to the second world war and there is still evidence of the many gun emplacements and other defences. The nearby WWII army camp has now become the interesting Muckleborough Collection - Britain's largest working military collection.

23 Sheringham

Sheringham claims to be "North Norfolk's Premier Seaside Town" - there is no doubt that it has many virtues and has much to offer its visitors beyond the beach. If it is the beach that is your main reason for visiting the town, then you should be aware that at high tide the sand is covered, leaving only a strip of pebbles. At low water a large area of sand is exposed, allowing you to have a most enjoyable day out participating in the full range of beach activities. RNLI lifeguards patrol a designated section of the beach. A promenade extends both eastwards and westwards from the main access point from the town centre, providing easy access to all parts of the beach. The centre of Sheringham with a good selection of cafés and shops is close to the beach.

23 Sheringham

If you leave Sheringham heading eastwards on the cliff top path you should be prepared for a steep climb as you ascend the 63m high Beeston Bump, which has a triangulation point at the top and provides excellent views in every direction. As you then descend you will pass the Beeston Regis Nature

Trail, with a number of pictorial display boards which show the flora and fauna to be found in the area. You can follow the path all the way to West Runton via the village of Beeston Regis. The cliff top path heading westwards takes you past the Sheringham golf course.

23 Sheringham

Sheringham has much to offer beyond the beach, including the North Norfolk Steam Railway which runs from Sheringham to Holt stopping at Weybourne and Kelling Heath Park. There is an excellent model boat pool on the Esplanade above the cliffs and you should visit the Fisherman's Heritage

Centre which houses an old rowing lifeboat. The Little Theatre has many excellent productions, including a first rate summer repertory theatre. A good time to visit Sheringham is during one of their famous 1940's weekends.

24 West Runton

West Runton is famous for the prehistoric elephant found and excavated from the cliffs in the 1990's. The West Runton Elephant is the oldest and largest fossil elephant skeleton ever to have been found in Britain, it would have stood 4m high and weighed 10 tonnes (twice that of a modern African

elephant). The cliff strata in which it was found is an exposed part of a 1.5m thick fresh water bed, making West Runton one of the best areas for fossil collecting. The beach has a large area of stones creating interesting rock pools and the Norfolk Wildlife Trust organises rock pooling in the summer, which is very popular with children. Swimming is best carried out at low water when an area of hard stone free sand is exposed.

24 West Runton

The beach is reached from the centre of West Runton by turning off the A149 into Water Lane. There is a large grassy cliff top car park and a concrete slope down to the beach, which passes toilets and a café. The walk from the car park along the cliff top to Sheringham is highly recommended, as it takes

you over Beeston Bump with spectacular views and past the Beeston Regis nature trail. However you should not try to walk along the beach to either Sheringham or East Runton unless you are sure of the tides, as you risk being cut off at high tide. As elsewhere the cliffs are eroding and this 6m high sea stack is east of West Runton.

25 East Runton

East Runton is on the A149 coast road west of Cromer. There is a short slope down to the beach from the cliff top car park and so it is popular with families who need to carry a lot of paraphernalia from their car. The beach is a mix of sand and stones. Presently there is a wide strip of large stones which can make swimming difficult at high tide, although the amount of sand and the exposure of the stones can change after a single storm and spring tide. When the tide recedes, a large area of stone free hard sand is exposed and this is the best time for bathing.

East Runton is popular with surfers and canoeists because of the easy access to the beach from the car park and the waves always seem a bit bigger than further along the coast at Cromer. The cliff top at East Runton is full of caravans and so there is neither a cliff top path to Cromer or to West Runton.

On the A149 as it passes through the village are a couple of pubs, a general store and an excellent outdoor shop called the Kit Bag. The centre of the village is just to the south of the coast road and has two village greens with ponds.

26 Cromer (West)

Cromer is the quintessential seaside town with its pier and traditional end of the pier summer show. The west beach is a mix of sand and stone and rock pools are exposed at low water. There are only a few places on the Norfolk coast where you can find rock pools and they are popular with children of all ages. Swimming is easier at low water when the sea goes beyond the area of stones and when extensive areas of hard sand are exposed. The most popular part of the beach is from the pier to the end of the promenade, which is protected by RNLI lifeguards. Other people go further along the beach in the direction of East Runton, where there are fewer rocks to inhibit swimming and the beach is quieter. Cromer beaches were awarded a Blue Flag in 2008.

The promenade behind the beach incorporates an amusement arcade, children's rides, beach huts, seafood and ice cream kiosks and disabled parking from where there is a good view of the beach and sea. The wooden beach huts are privately owned, but the brick built huts belong to North

Norfolk District Council and there are usually some available for short term hire. The road train travels between the cliff top car park and the pier via the town and the return journey is a good way of avoiding the steep climb back up the cliff steps.

26 Cromer (West)

Cromer is on a north facing coast and it is claimed that it has the only pleasure pier from which you can watch the sun both rise and set over the sea. We were fortunate to be in Cromer on carnival day and the highlight was the spectacular display by the Red Arrows.

26 Cromer (West)

The large Runton Road cliff top car park provides parking and a pleasant grassy picnic area. On a clear day it is a good place from which to watch both the local crab fishermen in action and larger ships as they make their way down the coast. The closest access to the promenade and beach is via a

zig-zag slope, or you can take the road train directly to the pier. On the cliff top are gardens and a putting green and nearby is a small boating lake. The town centre with its narrow streets is close to the seafront directly opposite the pier and is well worth a visit.

27 Cromer (East)

Cromer is described as "The Gem of the Norfolk Coast" and few can disagree with this claim. It is an unspoilt traditional small seaside town and is perfect for both day visits and longer holidays. The beach to the east of the pier nestles below the town and the imposing Hotel de Paris. The beach is a mixture of

sand and pebbles and is relatively small at high tide, but at low water the tide recedes to create an area of wet sand which enhances the enjoyment of the beach. The beach stretches eastwards below cliffs, which progressively rise to 62m and provide panoramic views of the pier and beach from the cliff top path. During the week leading up to the carnival, the east beach is the focal point of various activities for children, including sandcastle building competitions and a treasure hunt.

27 Cromer (East)

One of our visits to Cromer coincided with the RNLI lifeboat day when the new Tamar class lifeboat was put through its paces, along with inshore lifeboats and the rescue helicopter. Children were impressed with members of the crew who were dressed in both modern and old lifeboat attire. The Henry

Blogg RNLI lifeboat museum is on the east beach and has the Rocket café above it. A statue of Henry Blogg, a previous coxswain of the lifeboat who won the George Cross and three gold and four silver gallantry medals, overlooks the beach from the cliff top.

27 Cromer (East)

Cromer is synonymous with crabs and the opportunity should be taken to sample one during your visit. The crab boats are kept on the east beach and are launched and recovered, usually singlehandedly, with a variety of rusty old tractors.

27 Cromer (East)

Everyone who visits Cromer should take a leisurely stroll along the pier and children will find crab fishing from the sides irresistible. The church is claimed to have the highest tower in Norfolk at 50m and it is certainly worth the climb for the spectacular views both seaward and inland. The town centre is only a

short walk from the pier and east beach, where there is a museum housed within a Victorian fisherman's cottage. Above the cliffs behind east beach is North Lodge Park, which has well tended gardens, a putting green and model boat pool.

28 Cromer - Happy Valley

The main photograph may not look like a beach and indeed it is not. It shows a most spectacular swathe of wildflowers on the cliff top above the beach, in the area known as Happy Valley. The area has been seeded with a cornfield wild flower mix including cornflower, corn cockle poppy, corn marigold and

camomile and the result in August was spectacular. Also on the cliff top at this point is a working lighthouse. The beach is accessed by more than two hundred steps down the cliffs, which are very high at this

point. The beach, which is sandy with some stones, is usually quiet even at peak times. This is not surprising given that the return up the cliff steps provides excellent aerobic exercise, although you can avoid this by walking westward along the beach to Cromer. Happy Valley can be reached directly by a footpath off the Overstrand Road (B1159) on the eastern edge of Cromer. The footpath is opposite the turning into Cliff Road and is well signed.

28 Cromer - Happy Valley

Happy Valley and the beach are best seen as part of a circular walk. This can start at Cromer by following the cliff top path above the east beach until you reach Happy Valley. The steps down to the beach from the cliff top can easily be missed as they are hidden within the extensive vegetation. Before

descending the steps, you may wish to go beyond them to the highest point, where the lighthouse is situated and the views are well worth the extra energy expended. The alternative circular walk is to start at the cliff top car park at Overstrand and take the path westward. This passes alongside the Royal Cromer golf course and the path down to the beach is beyond the highest point. This walk is about twice as far as starting from Cromer, at around 8km.

29 Overstrand

Overstrand is a pleasant village with a wide sandy beach and safe swimming. The attractiveness of this area of the Norfolk coast and surrounding country side was extolled by Clement Scott the drama critic of the Daily Telegraph in the late 1800's. As a result, a number of wealthy people built holiday homes

in Overstrand and it became known as the village of millionaires. Three of the buildings were designed by the architect Edwin Lutyens and gardens were designed by Gertrude Jekll. The area became known as Poppyland because of the profusion of poppies.

The beach is reached by turning off the B1159 into the village and following the signs. The beach is accessed down a long slope to a promenade. There is a grassy beach top car park and toilets. The westward cliff top path starts at the car park and takes you alongside a golf course to the lighthouse and then

onward to Cromer. There is an excellent cliff top café which we can highly recommend. There is also an interesting hotel called the Seamarge where Winston Churchill reportedly stayed. Several North Sea gas platforms can be seen on the horizon.

30 Trimingham

Access to the beach at Trimingham was difficult to find, in fact we were not sure if there was an official access point, given that the cliffs here are reported to be the highest in Norfolk. There is a signed access to the beach, but it is very difficult because the path and steps have been lost due to slippage. The sign at the top warns you of this and you should certainly only attempt it on a fine day.

The beach is reached by taking a path from a lay by on the B1159 on the western edge of the village. The path takes you through a small wood to the top of the steps (or what remains of them) down to the beach. There is also a path diagonally across a corn field to the cliff top. The crops had been sown

right up to the edge and so great care should be taken as you approach the unguarded cliff edge. The sea comes right up to the cliffs at high tide, so you should be extremely careful not to become cut off. A landmark in Trimingham is the distinctive radar dome.

31 Mundesley

Mundesley is a large village located at a dip in the cliffs on the B1159 and so the access slope to the sandy beach is fairly short. It is a popular holiday destination for those who are looking for a traditional non commercialised seaside holiday. There are RNLI lifeguards on duty in the summer, as well as a Coastwatch station and also there is the independent Mundesley Volunteer Inshore Lifeboat.

31 Mundesley

Mundesley is one of only three places in Norfolk to have achieved Blue Flag status in 2008 for the excellence of its beach, in terms of water quality and safety. The entrance to a large car park is opposite the gardens and the beach access slope.

32 Bacton

When we visited Bacton we were pleased to find that the terminal for the Interconnector gas pipeline did not impact on the beach or the village. It is a large installation to the west of the village, but is not even seen from most parts of the beach and it appears not to produce any emissions. At low water the beach is wide and sandy but is mostly covered at high water.

Behind the beach is a concrete sea defence with a wide apron that acts as a promenade and extends for the full distance of the Bacton sea frontage and beach. Above this is a grassy embankment along which there is also a footpath. For the most part the sea front is either caravan parks or houses on private roads. There are several beach access points, the main one being at the western end of the beach, but one problem is car parking. North Norfolk District Council has built a large public car park at this end of the village, but when we visited in July it had not opened. It was still not open in January 2009 and NNDC were unable to advise when it would eventually open.

33 Walcott

At Walcott the B1159 runs parallel with the beach and the sea defence wall. Parking is allowed along the road at this point, with some beach facing parking at the eastern end and so access to the beach could not be easier. The sea comes right up to the wall at high spring tides and we understand

that the road has to be closed in stormy conditions. Walcott is a popular destination and parking places along the road can become full. One attraction on this road is the Kingfisher Fish Bar which we were told has excellent fish and chips.

34 Happisburgh

Happisburgh is the village that has been the most affected by cliff erosion and it continues to be a problem, with residents constantly battling with the authorities to try and get more investment in sea defences. Over the last 15 years some 25 properties have been lost, as the wooden sea defences built

in the late 50's have been failing. The ramp down to the beach was destroyed a few years ago and the lifeboat has had to be relocated along the coast to Cart Gap. Access to the beach from the cliff top and campsite is now via a staircase on a steel tower.

34 Happisburgh

There appears to be an excellent community spirit in Happisburgh which has not only been brought together by their problem of erosion, but in 1990 they saved their lighthouse from closure. It is the oldest working lighthouse in East Anglia and the only independently run lighthouse in Great Britain. In 1990 it was repainted during the filming of "Challenge Anneka" and is maintained

and operated by voluntary contributions. It is open to the public on certain days in the summer. Happisburgh has excellent beaches and a convenient cliff top car park, so a visit to support the local community is worthwhile.

35 Eccles-on-Sea

Eccles has been badly affected by the sea over the past centuries. In 1604 Eccles was all but destroyed by a ferocious storm when only 14 houses remained. In 1895 St Mary's church finally succumbed to the sea. Today it is made up of a few private roads and pre-war bungalows known as the

Bush Estate, which is protected from the sea by sand dunes. The two main access points to the fine beach are at either end of the Bush Estate. At the western end is Cart Gap where there is large public car park and to where the Happisburgh lifeboat has been relocated.

The beach to the east of Eccles is accessed through North Gap and has more soft sand than Cart Gap. North Gap is at the end of Beach Road and is reached from the village of Lessingham, but there is no car park and only a limited amount of road side parking. Cart Gap, where there is parking, is at the end of Cart Gap Road, a turning close to the village of Whimpwell Green.

36 Sea Palling

This beach was a surprise to us. A huge sandy bay with a fine beach backed by sand dunes, it is clearly a popular destination for those who know of the well kept secret that is Sea Palling. The excellent beaches of Sea Palling have come about because of a beach reclamation and a sea defence scheme carried out in 1995. This involved the construction of nine reefs just offshore. As well as providing flood protection, they are allowing the sand to build up forming bays within the reefs. These now provide sheltered and safe areas for bathing and boating.

36 Sea Palling

The reefs which are constructed from large stones have allowed the formation of rock pools which are extremely popular with children, although signs warn of the dangers of climbing on the rocks. Sea Palling beach is one of only three beaches in Norfolk to have been awarded a Blue Flag for water

and beach quality in 2008. The beach has RNLI lifeguards in the summer and an independently run lifeboat operated by the Palling Volunteer Rescue Service. There is ramp for launching small boats and jet skis. Sun loungers can be hired on the beach.

36 Sea Palling

Sea Palling is on the B1159 about four miles from Stalham. It has a large car park to accommodate the influx of summer visitors. There are two pubs with restaurants, an amusement arcade and a playing field with picnic tables.

37 Waxham

There is an access path to the beach through the high sand dunes from the small village of Waxham on the B1159. There is no official parking area, just a limited amount of unofficial parking in the lane leading to the Waxham Access and consequently the beach will always be sparsely populated even at peak times. The western part of the beach is opposite the most easterly of the nine reefs extending from Sea Palling. The beach at Waxham is excellent and has no doubt benefitted from the effect of the reefs and other work carried out in the 1990's.

37 Waxham

The main feature of the small village is the Waxham Great Barn, which is the longest in Norfolk and was built in the 1580's. Within the barn is an audio tour, an exhibition and an interactive area for children. Alongside the barn is the Tea Lounge café, built within a converted cow shed.

38 Waxham Sands

There is access to a fine sandy beach over the sand dunes from the Waxham Sands Holiday Park, the entrance of which is on the B1159 two miles east of Waxham Barns. Waxham Sands has facilities for tents and touring caravans and welcomes day visitors to use their car park and the beach access.

38 Waxham Sands

39 Horsey

There are two ways to reach the stretch of beach at Horsey. The first is from the car park at the Horsey Warren Nature Reserve and a path through the high ridge of sand dunes known as Horsey Gap. The turning is off the B1159 about half a mile west of Horsey village. It is not well signed but is close to the Poppyland tea room.

The area between the road and the beach at Horsey Gap is managed by the National Trust and is part of the Winterton to Horsey Dunes Site of Special Scientific Interest. Horsey is the closest Broadland village to the coast.

The second way to reach the beach is to walk directly from the village. The mile long track starts at the Nelson Head pub. A good time to visit the beach here is in November and December when the colony of Grey seals are giving birth to their single white pups on the beach. At this time the beach is roped off and a viewing platform is provided so you can observe the seals at close quarters. We actually visited on a frosty day in early January when there were only a few pups left on the beach. We followed it with an excellent lunch by a log fire in the pub.

40 Winterton-on-Sea

The extensive sandy beach at Winterton-on-Sea is backed by high sand dunes and a large area of dune heath and grasslands that extend to Horsey and form the Winterton Dunes National Nature Reserve. This area which is designated as an SSSI is privately owned and managed by English Nature and is home to a wide range of species including the Natterjack toad. 110 species of moths have been recorded here.

Access to the beach is from the B1159 through the attractive village of Winterton. At the beach there is a large grassy car park on the edge of the Dunes Nature Reserve, with parking that overlooks the sea. As does the terrace of the Dunes Café. Also on the edge of the dunes are the distinctive thatched roundhouses of the Hermanus holiday centre.

41 Hemsby

Hemsby's was one of the busiest and most popular beaches that we visited, with lots of holiday makers from the many holiday and chalet parks that are a situated between the village and the beach. However the wide sandy beach which is backed with high sand dunes was not overcrowded. A unique feature of Hemsby is ice cream vans and donut stalls actually on the beach.

41 Hemsby

In Beach Road there are numerous amusement arcades and gift shops. There is a large car park and an amusement park on the landward side of the sand dunes. The access to the beach is along a boardwalk, although there are other unofficial paths through the sand dunes.

42 Newport

Newport is directly to the south of Hemsby and is in effect joined to it. We could not find a public car park, so presumably the beach here is used mainly by people who live or are holidaying in Newport. It is a wide sandy beach backed by huge sand dunes. Hemsby beach can be seen in the distance.

We found one path over the sand dunes to the beach from St Mary's Road which runs parallel to the beach, presumably there are others.

43 Scratby

The main access to the beach at Scratby is down a slope and steps from a small car park (with toilets) on Rottenstone Lane. This is a road that runs between the coast and a large caravan park. There are good sea views from the car park, but we would imagine that it quickly becomes full in the summer. At this point the beach is relatively narrow and has a row of large boulders which have been positioned to prevent erosion of high sand dunes which have virtually become cliffs at this point. The beach is soft sand and is popular with those staying at the nearby caravan park.

43 Scratby

As you head northwards on the beach, the large sea defence stones end and the beach widens. You can also walk in this direction on a pleasant path along the cliff tops. Signs say that it is private land but advise that you are allowed to walk across it. There are a number of paths down to the beach from here.

44 California

The small village of California apparently owes its name to the discovery of 16th century gold coins on the beach in 1848. This was at the time of the Californian gold rush in American and so the new village was given the same name. The beach is reached by turning into California Road from the B1159 Scratby Road. There is no public car park and so the beach is most appropriate for those staying at the local holiday parks. The California Tavern Pub has a large car park for use by its patrons. Access to the beach is via steps down the sandy cliff.

45 Caister-on-Sea

In one respect Caister-on-Sea is in the shadow of Great Yarmouth being only three miles to the north, but it certainly has its own identity. Not least because it dates back to Roman times, being one of the oldest settlements in Norfolk. The remains of a Roman wall, gateway and buildings can still be seen

in Caister. It has a wide sandy beach with some stony parts and some large rocks. The sea view is dominated by the Scroby Sands wind farm. There is a car park close to the beach and a café on the beach with a decked terrace where you can sit and take in the sea air.

From the number of boats it would seem that Caister is still an active fishing village. Caister also has a lifeboat station with a long history of heroic rescues. In 1969 the RNLI decided to close the station, but an independent lifeboat has continued to operate from Caister thanks to local support.

46 Great Yarmouth (North)

Great Yarmouth is one of the best known seaside resorts in the country and certainly the most popular in Norfolk. We were probably typical in that we knew Yarmouth for its fun parks rather than its beaches and so were surprised to find just how superb the beaches are. The beach north of Britannia Pier has

soft sand and is very wide, consequently it appeared to be sparsely populated. There are some children's activities on the beach and a wide and long promenade. Nearby are shops, ice cream stalls and a visitor centre for the Scroby Sands wind farm.

As you head northwards the beach becomes even wider with an extensive area of sand dunes developing. Attractive gardens and a large boating lake run parallel with the promenade and beach, although only a smaller lake for pedal boats seems to be in use.

47 Great Yarmouth (South)

Much of Great Yarmouth's South Beach is hidden from view by the many attractions on the "Golden Mile", including the famous Pleasure Beach fun park. However once you have ventured on to the beach, you cannot help but be impressed by the huge sandy beach that stretches out in front of you.

47 Great Yarmouth (South)

47 Great Yarmouth (South)

As you head south beyond the Pleasure Beach fun park, the beach becomes more remote with extensive areas of sand dunes. Ultimately you come to the area where the new harbour is being constructed. We were previously unaware of Nelson's Monument in the southern part of Great Yarmouth and plan to return on one of its open days.

47 Great Yarmouth (South)

We cannot begin to touch on the many attractions for visitors to Great Yarmouth and which make it one of the top holiday destinations in the UK. We can say however that it has the excellent beaches that you would expect to find at a top seaside resort.

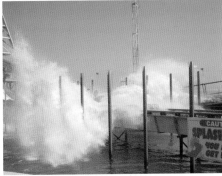

48 Gorleston-on-Sea (North)

We had never visited Gorleston before and so it came as a great surprise to find that it was such a thriving holiday resort with a superb sandy beach. The beach is within a sheltered bay formed by the South Pier at the entrance to the River Yare. Within the beach area is a children's paddling pool and a model boating pool, as well as a bouncy castle and a carousel.

49 Gorleston-on-Sea (South)

As you head south on Gorleston beach it becomes much quieter. Although it remains wide, sandy and fully accessible, with a wide promenade which continues up to the point where the beach coincides with the cliff top golf course.

49 Gorleston-on-Sea (South)

The area behind the southern part of the beach has been developed to encourage exercise and fitness. The local authority has created measured walks on the promenade and the upper level. The 2705m "Heart & Soles" walk should take between 25 and 34 minutes depending on your level of fitness. There is also the Mia-Lucy Rose Trim Park, created in memory of a young lady who tragically lost her life while on a round the world trip.

50 Hopton-on-Sea

Hopton is the last beach in Norfolk or of course the first if you are travelling from Suffolk. Signs say that you cannot walk along either the beach or the cliff top to the first Suffolk village of Corton, we assume that this is for practical reasons rather than border controls! The beach is pleasantly sandy with some stones and for much of its length there is a wooden sea defence structure.

Behind the beach are low grassy cliffs and virtually all of the sea frontage is taken up by the two holiday parks, Hopton Holiday Village and Potters Leisure Resort, both of which have their own beach access. There appears to be just two public access points to the beach, one is a path to the north of the Hopton Holiday Village. This ends with steps down to the beach. The other is via Beach Road, a narrow lane between the two resorts which ends in a steep slope to the beach. Neither has any nearby car parking.

Epilogue

Well that's it, the beaches of Norfolk. We hope that we have inspired you to visit the Norfolk coast if you have never been here before, or to go beyond your regular or local beaches if you live locally. As you will have seen we are not professional photographers and so the colours have not been doctored or the images enhanced in anyway. The blues of the sea and sky are exactly as we photographed them, as are the greys resulting from the few dull days.

We apologise in advance for any errors or omissions and we would welcome any feedback to incorporate in the next edition. Perhaps you can also help us to solve two mysteries -

Who is collecting shoes - mainly odd - and placing them on a pallet at Blakeney Point?

What is this? It was seen on the shingle bank at Salthouse. Sawn sections of tree trunk had been placed inside - presumably as seats .

USEFUL LINKS

www.norfolkwildlifetrust.org.uk

www.rspb.org.uk

www.nationaltrust.org.uk

www.english-nature.org.uk

www.rnli.co.uk

www.nationaltrail.co.uk

www.literarynorfolk.co.uk

www.holkham.co.uk

www.northnorfolk.org

www.norfolkbiodiversity.org

www.theukcoastalzone.com

www.ramsar.org

www.natura.org

www.norfolk-lavender.co.uk

www.hunstanton-on-line.co.uk

www.visitwestnorfolk.com

www.west-norfolk.gov.uk

www.ukfossils.co.uk

www.norfolkcoast.co.uk

www.norfolksmugglers.co.uk

www.wellsguide.com

www.bbc.co.uk/norfolk

www.cromertown.org

www.experiencesheringham.co.uk

www.nnrailway.co.uk

www.museums.norfolk.gov.uk

www.tournorfolk.co.uk

www.happisburgh.org.uk

MORE USEFUL LINKS

www.esfjc.co.uk

www.wellsharbourrailway.com

www.salthousehistory.co.uk

www.happisburgh.org.uk

www.seapalling.com

www.hemsbyparishcouncil.org.uk

www.nelsonmonument.org.uk

www.norfolkbroads.com

www.great-yarmouth.gov.uk

www.gorleston-heritage.co.uk

www.muckleburgh.co.uk

www.bishopsboats.com

www.nci.org.uk

ACKNOWLEDGEMENTS

To our family for their encouragement and for providing us with the grandchildren who helped us to enjoy many of the beaches. To Mark for technical advice.

To the Holkham Estate for permission to photograph the beaches at Holkham and Wells. To all the organisations mentioned in the book who are doing a great job in caring for and enhancing the Norfolk coast.